Justice
for All

Members of the Brookings Task Force on Civil Justice Reform

Justice for All

Reducing Costs and Delay in Civil Litigation

Report of a Task Force

The Brookings Institution
Washington, D.C.

Copyright © 1989 by

THE BROOKINGS INSTITUTION

1775 Massachusetts Avenue, N.W.

Washington, D.C. 20036

Library of Congress Catalog Card Number: 89-85763

ISBN 0-8157-5277-6

9 8 7 6 5 4 3 2 1

THE BROOKINGS INSTITUTION is an independent organization devoted to nonpartisan research, education, and publication in economics, government, foreign policy, and the social sciences generally. Its principal purposes are to aid in the development of sound public policies and to promote public understanding of issues of national importance.

The Institution was founded on December 8, 1927, to merge the activities of the Institute for Government Research, founded in 1916, the Institute of Economics, founded in 1922, and the Robert Brookings Graduate School of Economics and Government, founded in 1924.

The Board of Trustees is responsible for the general administration of the Institution, while the immediate direction of the policies, program, and staff is vested in the President, assisted by an advisory committee of the officers and staff. The by-laws of the Institution state: "It is the function of the Trustees to make possible the conduct of scientific research, and publication, under the most favorable conditions, and to safeguard the independence of the research staff in the pursuit of their studies and in the publication of the results of such studies. It is not a part of their function to determine, control, or influence the conduct of particular investigations or the conclusions reached."

The President bears the final responsibility for the decision to publish a manuscript as a Brookings book. In reaching his judgment on the competence, accuracy, and objectivity of each study, the President is advised by the director of the appropriate research program and weighs the views of a panel of expert outside readers who report to him in confidence on the quality of the work. Publication of a work signifies that it is deemed a competent treatment worthy of public consideration but does not imply endorsement of conclusions or recommendations.

The Institution maintains its position of neutrality on issues of public policy in order to safeguard the intellectual freedom of the staff. Hence interpretations or conclusions in Brookings publications should be understood to be solely those of the authors and should not be attributed to the Institution, to its trustees, officers, or other staff members, or to the organizations that support its research.

FOREWORD

The American system of civil justice is under attack: from clients who believe that their cases take too long to get to trial and cost far too much; from federal and state legislators who hear these complaints from their constituents; from judges who must manage the system; and from many attorneys themselves who participate in it.

At the suggestion of the chairman of the Senate Judiciary Committee, Senator Joseph R. Biden, Jr., the Brookings Institution and the Foundation for Change convened a task force of authorities from throughout the United States to develop a set of recommendations to alleviate the problems of excessive cost and delay. The task force comprised leading litigators from the plaintiffs' and defense bar, civil and women's rights lawyers, attorneys representing consumer and environmental organizations, representatives of the insurance industry, general counsels of major corporations, former judges, and law professors. The members of the group met six times between September 1988 and June 1989. They were assisted throughout by staff members from the Institute for Civil Justice at the Rand Corporation (led by Deborah Hensler), by Senate Judiciary Committee staff, and by other experts, including current federal judges, leading attorneys, and law professors. Financial and administrative support for the meetings was provided by both the Brookings Institution and the Foundation for Change.

This report is the product of the group's efforts. It was drafted primarily by the group's reporters, Robert E. Litan, a senior fellow in the Economic Studies program at Brookings, and Mark Gitenstein, executive director of the Foundation for Change. The final report, however, was reviewed by and speaks for the entire group.

The report concentrates on flaws in and solutions for the federal civil justice system only. Nevertheless, the analysis and conclusions may apply to many states and localities. Indeed, reforms already adopted in state and municipal courts served as models for specific recommendations advanced by the task force.

The task force report suggests ways of reducing costs and delays. Congress should encourage constructive change of procedural rules by directing each federal district court to develop, with assistance from its local bar, a "Civil Justice Reform Plan" to provide greater discipline on both attorneys and judges. The report outlines several concrete measures that should be included in these plans.

Judges need to be more involved in the discovery phase of litigation and, whatever assistance they may enlist, must remain ultimately responsible for managing it. The group's suggestions for procedural changes should make it easier for judges to speed up discovery and, where appropriate, to encourage settlement.

Clients, especially those in the corporate sector, can be encouraged to do a better job of managing their outside counsel. At the same time, attorneys can do a better job of managing their cases. Again, the procedural changes the group recommends should provide better incentives for both clients and their attorneys to act in ways more consistent with the broader public interest in achieving the just and efficient resolution of disputes.

The task force members are grateful to all those who assisted in this pioneering effort. Special thanks are due to David Griffith, who provided research assistance, and Victor M. Alfaro, who verified the accuracy of the facts and citations.

This report was supported financially in part by Aetna Life and Casualty Foundation, the Association of Trial Lawyers of America, and Whittaker Corporation. It represents solely the views of the members of the group and not necessarily those of the trustees, officers, or staff members of the Brookings Institution.

BRUCE K. MACLAURY
President

September 1989
Washington, D.C.

CONTENTS

OVERVIEW

Whether we have too many cases or too few, or even, miraculously, precisely the right number, there can be little doubt that the system is not working very well. Too many cases take too much time to be resolved and impose too much cost upon litigants and taxpayers alike.

Jon O. Newman, "Rethinking Fairness"

The United States has long been admired throughout the world for its sophisticated and well-developed system of civil justice, which is designed to guarantee all citizens the opportunity to resolve disputes peaceably before a jury of their peers in a court overseen by impartial judicial officers. Indeed, the United States can be proud that it affords legal protections to victims of injustice—protections that are provided through litigation and the court system.

But increasingly, all who participate in the judicial system—litigants, judges, and attorneys—are voicing complaints about its inefficiency and lack of fairness. In many courts, litigants must wait for years to resolve their disputes. In the meantime, their attorneys pursue ever more expensive means of discovery to prepare for trial, often having to duplicate their preparation when trial dates are postponed. Among the bulk of cases that are never tried but settled, many are overprepared and overdiscovered. In short, civil litigation costs too much and takes too long.

The high costs of litigation burden everyone. Our businesses spend too much on legal expenses at a time when they are confronted with increasingly intense international competition. They pass those costs on to consumers, who then pay unnecessarily high prices for the products and services they buy. People who take their cases to court or who must defend themselves against legal actions often face staggering legal bills and years of delay.

1

This situation need not—and must not—continue. There is broad consensus within the legal community that meaningful reforms can reduce the expenses and delay involved in civil litigation. Procedural rules can be changed to provide much stronger incentives to parties and their attorneys to bring to court only those matters that cannot be resolved through other means and, once in court, to resolve those disputes, whether by settlement or trial, more quickly and inexpensively. At the same time, all the actors in the litigation system can and must play more active roles in solving its problems.

The task force recognizes that its efforts are hardly the first to tackle the dual problems of litigation costs and delay and the overall condition of the civil justice system. As early as 1906, Dean Roscoe Pound lamented that the "effect of our exaggerated contentious procedure is not only to irritate parties, witnesses and jurors . . . but to give the whole community a false notion of the purpose and end of law" (Pound, reprinted 1964, p. 282). Seventy years later, at a conference named after Dean Pound, problems in the civil justice system were again recognized to be severe. (See Erickson, 1978.) And in the past decade, numerous individuals and groups have carefully examined the discovery process, the management of cases by judges, and a host of other important civil justice issues. The American Bar Association, the Association of Trial Lawyers of America, and the American Law Institute, to name just a few, have all made important contributions to improving the efficiency of the civil justice system while maintaining the essential requirements of justice and fairness.[1]

This report builds upon these efforts, but we believe it is unique in a significant respect. Specifically, it grows out of an extensive series of discussions among a broad spectrum of experts and participants in the civil justice system in the United States: private attorneys representing plaintiffs and defendants; general counsels of major corporations; attorneys representing civil and women's rights, and consumer and environmental organizations; represen-

---

1. Even at this writing, the Federal Courts Study Committee, chaired by Judge Joseph Weis, is carefully studying a variety of issues pertaining to the operation of the federal courts, and the members of the task force look forward to the committee's report.

tatives of the insurance industry; former judges; and law professors. On many legal and policy matters, the participants in our task force disagree. However, on the condition of our civil justice system and on the means of improving it, the members of our task force find common ground.

The excessive cost and delay associated with litigating civil cases in America should no longer be tolerated and can be forcefully addressed through procedural reform, more active case management by judges, and better efforts by attorneys and their clients to control cost and delay.

In particular, we conclude:

—That Congress should require each federal district court to develop its own "Civil Justice Reform Plan" that should include, among other things, provisions for assigning cases of differing degrees of complexity to different "tracks"; mandatory initial conferences in most cases to schedule discovery and trial and to explore the desirability of alternative techniques for dispute resolution; early, firm trial dates for all cases; firm time guidelines for the discovery phase of cases; and procedures for resolving motions quickly. Districts with significant case backlogs should outline in their plans procedures for reducing those backlogs.

—That judges should take a more active role in managing their cases, ending the practice in some courts of delegating to magistrates functions that are in fact better performed by judges. At the same time, the federal judiciary must be given more resources to do its job: resources to computerize its administrative support system to bring it into the modern age, to raise judicial salaries, and to spread information about effective judicial management techniques through enhanced judicial training upon confirmation and through enhanced continuing education. In addition, current judicial vacancies should be filled expeditiously and requests for more judges in certain districts with substantial case backlogs carefully reviewed.

—That the professional bar and clients should place much greater emphasis on reducing litigation costs and delay and take measures to accomplish this objective.

We focus in this report primarily on the problems of cost and delay in the federal courts and on solutions we believe will alleviate

3

these problems. However, there is much to be done as well in state and local courts—where the dockets are as crowded, if not more crowded, than at comparable federal courts. Still, procedural innovations by state and local courts that have reduced costs and delays around the country have much to teach federal policymakers. We apply their lessons in framing the recommendations outlined later in the report.

We recognize that many of our recommendations have been advanced before by other groups and experts who have studied our civil justice system. Indeed, many of our procedural suggestions have already been implemented in some form by certain federal judges across the country. But it is precisely because a consensus about meaningful reform measures appears to have emerged that we believe the time is ripe for more systematic efforts to be undertaken by Congress, the judiciary, and the legal community and its clients to reduce costs and delay in our legal system.

THE PROBLEM

This task force has come together out of the belief, borne out by the collective experience of its members, that the problems of cost and delay in our civil justice system are serious and in need of immediate attention by all those who participate in and are affected by it. That this report has been produced at all by individuals with diverse, and often adverse, courtroom interests is powerful evidence by itself that there is strong dissatisfaction with the way civil justice in the United States now works.

Representatives of corporate defendants and insurance companies in our group believe that the rising costs of litigation are draining valuable resources from the essential functions of American business: making better products and delivering quality services at the lowest possible cost. Expensive litigation not only hits the bottom line, cutting into profits, but also diverts the time and energy of corporate officials from their business responsibilities. They are instead forced to respond to discovery requests and to prepare for and testify at depositions, hearings, and trials. While much litigation cannot be avoided, our corporate and insurance representatives believe that resolving it at lower cost is clearly in the interest of American business and of the public at large.

Although generally on the opposite side of the courtroom, representatives of civil rights, consumer, environmental, and other public interest groups on our task force agree that the civil justice system must be reformed. The higher the cost and the longer the delay—problems that certain business and insurance interests make worse through their own delay and discovery tactics—the more difficult it can be for aggrieved parties to obtain timely and proper judicial relief. Accordingly, many people have found that they are unable to make effective use of the courts to resolve their disputes. Meanwhile, many others who are in the system are often compelled by the high costs and delay to settle early for less than satisfactory amounts (Bok, 1983). At a time when many citizens and groups are turning to the courts to redress what they believe to be serious wrongs or injustices, cases must move as quickly and inexpensively as possible.

In short, high transactions costs—manifested in high out-of-pocket legal fees and the time consumed by delay—are the enemies of justice. This is understood by the lawyers who use our courts and the judges who preside over them. In connection with the activities of the task force, Louis Harris and Associates surveyed in mid-1988 more than a thousand participants in the civil justice system—private litigators representing plaintiffs and defendants, "public interest" litigators, corporate counsel, and federal district court judges.[2] The survey, conducted through in-depth telephone interviews, sought the respondents' opinions on a wide range of issues relating to transactions costs and delay. Despite the diversity of the people interviewed, several widely held views about the civil justice system emerged:

—More than half of the federal judges, corporate counsel, and public interest litigators surveyed believe that the costs of litigating civil cases in the United States today are a "major problem." Even 40 percent of private litigators hold this view. Those who have litigated abroad perceive U.S. litigation costs to be substantially higher than those in foreign countries. And a majority of corporate counsel and federal judges think that litigation costs, corrected for inflation, have increased "greatly" during the past decade.

—A majority of judges and lawyers agree that the high costs of litigating in America unreasonably impede access to the civil justice system by the ordinary citizen. Furthermore, they believe that the civil justice system today gives an unfair advantage to "large interests" with greater resources.

—The respondents agree that the most important cause of high litigation costs or delays is abuse by attorneys of the discovery process, which leads to "overdiscovery" of cases rather than to attempts to focus on controlling issues. Both plaintiffs' and defendants' attorneys share in the blame. Corporate counsel and private litigators estimate that 60 percent of all litigation costs in a typi-

2. The key findings of the survey are summarized here. For a full description of the survey findings, see Louis Harris and Associates (1989).

cal federal court case arise out of discovery. As Judge William Schwarzer has written elsewhere: "For many lawyers, discovery is a Pavlovian reaction. When a lawsuit is filed, and the filing stamp comes down, the word processor begins to grind out interrogatories and requests for production. Deposition notices drop like autumn leaves" (Schwarzer, 1989, p. 31).

—A majority of the lawyers and even the judges surveyed also believe that the "failure of judges to control the discovery process" is another important cause of high litigation costs.

Given the widespread dissatisfaction with the current system, one would expect those who participate in it to be pessimistic about the possibilities for implementing meaningful reforms. Surprisingly, the respondents to the Harris survey overwhelmingly agreed that such changes *can* be made and that, if implemented, would *significantly reduce* the costs of litigation.

Specifically, nearly all of the lawyers surveyed, as well as eight out of ten federal judges, support procedural systems that put cases on different discovery and trial "tracks" based on complexity: the simpler the case, the faster the track. Consistent with this recommendation, almost 80 percent of the attorneys also favor an eighteen-month limit on discovery, with provisions for exceptional circumstances. Both lawyers and judges overwhelmingly favor increasing the role of federal judges as active case managers, making greater use of pretrial and status conferences to monitor and limit discovery, and scheduling early and firm trial dates.

To summarize: there is a significant degree of consensus among those who regularly participate in the civil justice system about what reforms are most needed to reduce transactions costs and delays. This consensus was also reflected in our task force. The key reforms that we outline in detail below are consistent with those identified in the Harris survey.

RECOMMENDATIONS FOR
PROCEDURAL REFORM

More than fifty years have passed since the Federal Rules of Civil Procedure (FRCP) were drafted and adopted. As expressed in 1938, the core objectives of the rules are threefold: "the just, speedy and inexpensive determination of every action." With the passage of five decades, these objectives—set forth in Rule 1, a symbol of their importance that is all too often forgotten or ignored—have not changed. They are, and should be, fundamentally important and enduring. Our civil justice system should continue to strive for their delivery in every case.

What has changed during the past fifty years is not the objectives of the rules but the civil justice system itself—the number and kinds of cases, the litigants, and the lawyers. The civil rules, in other words, apply to a dramatically different system than that which existed at the time of their drafting. To some degree, the rules that follow Rule 1 have sought to keep pace with the changes in the system. The amendment process has been used on several occasions, most recently in 1980 and 1983, when changes were in large part directed at correcting abuses in the discovery process and increasing the involvement of judges in case management.

To a significant degree, however, the reform efforts of years past have been stopgaps designed to address narrow problems rather than to effect fundamental changes that would dramatically improve the system (Rosenberg, 1984). The rising costs and delays involved in litigation demand now a more far-reaching approach. Indeed, Justice Lewis Powell's dissent from the adoption of the 1980 amendments has been prophetic:

> I doubt that many judges or lawyers familiar with the proposed amendments believe they will have an appreciable effect on the acute problems . . . The Court's adoption of these inade-

8

quate changes could postpone effective reform for another decade . . . I do not dissent because the modest amendments recommended by the Judicial Conference are undesirable. *I simply believe that Congress' acceptance of these tinkering changes will delay for years the adoption of genuinely effective reforms* (Powell, 1980, pp. 522–23; emphasis added).

The task force believes that time has proven Justice Powell's 1980 prediction to be entirely correct. Although well intentioned, past changes in the rules failed to alleviate the dual problems of litigation costs and delays. Accordingly, we have concluded that reform efforts must look beyond "tinkering changes," in Justice Powell's words, and must instead search for more systemic solutions.

In developing the recommendations outlined below, we were mindful of many past efforts by distinguished bodies to accomplish the same or similar objectives. Accordingly, we made every effort to avoid reinventing the wheel. Instead, we borrowed freely from ideas that have been in the public domain for some time, as well as from successful experiments by many federal and state courts. In addition, we drew upon the findings of the Harris survey summarized earlier. At the same time, the wealth of experience and the diversity of backgrounds represented by members of the task force helped produce what we believe is an innovative and workable package of reform recommendations.

While all participants in the civil justice system—judges, attorneys, and their clients—clearly can and should make contributions to reducing delay and transactions costs, there is no substitute for structuring the procedural rules themselves to ensure that litigants have the proper *incentives* to achieve these objectives. Simple directives will not do and cannot be enforced. But the system can be better designed so that what is in the interest of each of the participants also serves the broader social interest of delivering justice fairly, efficiently, and expeditiously.

We have been mindful throughout our deliberations of the enormous challenges that federal judges must confront as the principal actors in the judicial system and of the difficulties they face. In many districts, judicial caseloads have substantially increased in both number and complexity. The processing of civil cases, in particular, is slowed by rising numbers of criminal cases, which in effect must be given priority in scheduling. Meanwhile, the judicial system continues to operate in horse-and-buggy fashion, while technology in nearly every other segment of our society races ahead. Ironically, though many of the attorneys who appear regularly in court work in offices equipped with the latest in computer and word processing technology, federal judges generally are short of computer facilities and other resources that could expedite their processing of cases.

We considered a wide range of suggestions and proposals for speeding up the disposition of cases in the federal civil justice system. Not all made our list of recommendations. For example, some have suggested that Congress must itself take the responsibility for revising the Federal Rules of Civil Procedure by requiring that all civil cases in all federal courts be subject to identical and strict time deadlines for discovery and trial. Others have urged that the definition of "relevant" evidence subject to discovery be tightened considerably. And there is support for the so-called English rule on attorneys' fees: losing parties pay the costs and fees expended by the winners.

These and certain other proposals failed to attract unanimous support within the task force for various reasons: either they were not perceived to be fair to all parties or effective versions could not be developed. Significantly, however, the members of the task force agreed on a range of other reforms that they believe will preserve the fairness objectives of our civil justice system while at the same time reducing both cost and delay.

Several important principles run through our specific procedural recommendations. First, the proposals recognize that the same set of generic procedures need not, and indeed should not, apply to all types of cases. As Professor Maurice Rosenberg has written:

> [The] conception that the ideal [of the just, speedy, and inexpensive resolution of disputes] is attainable by a monolithic set of rules applied to virtually all the varied types of civil actions filed in the federal district courts is a gallant

10

illusion that compounds the difficulties . . . Perfect process, worthy goal though it is, is not the way to produce prompt or inexpensive dispositions. Perfection can be suffocating if it makes the process more elaborate, complex and labor-intensive than the case can bear (Rosenberg, 1984, pp. 243, 247).

We believe the time has come to recognize that what should be considered "reasonable" or "regular" time and expense for case processing ought to reflect a fair appraisal—at the outset of the litigation—of its complexity. Assigning cases to a tracking system, probably organized into three tiers, would alter the inertia of the system and give parties and judge strong incentives to move cases along quickly to disposition.

Second, meeting reasonable time expectations will be impossible unless courts have both the resources and the will to implement them consistently and then to convey this clearly to all participants. Firm trial dates, associated discovery cutoff dates, and time limits for the disposition of motions provide clear warning of the system's expectations for each case. Limiting relief from those dates to legitimate "good cause" exceptions ensures flexibility while at the same time enforcing the reasonable expectations for the matter.

Third, our recommendations take account of the diversity of caseloads and types of litigations across different federal jurisdictions. Accordingly, we do not advocate the adoption of a uniform set of reform suggestions to be applied by all district courts throughout the nation. Nor do we believe it useful for Congress itself to make these judgments for the district courts.

Instead, reform must come from the "bottom up," or from those in each district who must live with the civil justice system on a regular basis. The proper role for Congress, we believe, is to launch this process with a mix of suggestions and incentives and then to let those who use the system fill in the details. Accordingly, our core recommendations allow each federal court, with assistance from its local bar and client community, to develop its own set of reforms for reducing delay and litigation costs within some broad parameters that Congress would establish through federal legislation.

PROCEDURAL RECOMMENDATION 1 : *By statute, direct all federal district courts to develop and implement within twelve months a "Civil Justice Reform Plan."*

The expense and delay patterns for civil cases vary across different federal district courts. In addition, the districts have developed different procedures and customs for handling their civil cases. To take advantage of the expertise reflected in these differences in approaches and procedures, as well as to avoid freezing in place a single set of case management procedures for all jurisdictions, the task force recommends that each district court be required to develop its own "Civil Justice Reform Plan," a step that certain districts already have undertaken. We further recommend that each district be required to submit its plan to the Federal Judicial Center (FJC) with a report explaining how it addressed the topics embodied in the other recommendations outlined here. Through its plan, each district court should seek to streamline discovery, improve judicial case management, and renew its commitment to the "just, speedy and inexpensive" resolution of civil disputes.

The Creation of a Planning Group with Membership from the Bench, the Public, and the Bar. In developing its plan, each district court should include in its planning group a representative magistrate in the district, public representatives, and lawyers practicing in firms and corporations representing each of the major categories of litigants in the district. The planning groups may vary in their membership, therefore, from district to district. The task force believes that the wide participation of those who use and are involved in the court system in each district will not only maximize the prospects that workable plans will be developed, but will also stimulate a much-needed dialogue between the bench, the bar, and client communities about methods for streamlining litigation practice.

Written Objectives. It is important, in this time of escalating litigation costs, for each district court to express its commitment to cost and delay reduction through written goals that will guide the processing and disposition of civil cases. Furthermore, each district should do everything it can to publicize its efforts to develop and adopt a plan. As costs and delays have mounted, the calls for greater accountability have increased as well. The kind of plan we have recommended can increase public awareness of the efforts of judges, lawyers, and litigants to improve the civil justice system.

Backup Model Plans. The task force recommends that if, at the end of one year, a district court has failed to develop and implement a plan, a model plan developed by the judicial council for its circuit should automatically go into effect. These model plans should be developed with public participation and should benefit from technical expertise provided by the Federal Judicial Center (discussed below). To ensure that model plans are ready for immediate implementation upon the failure of any district to carry out its own plan, we suggest that the judicial councils in each circuit begin developing their backup plans at the same time each district is charged with that task.

It is unlikely, of course, that backup plans will be necessary. We expect that the district courts would generally be enthusiastic about participating in a nationwide plan to reduce the costs and delays in the civil justice system. Moreover, we outline below a strong incentive for districts to comply: federal financial assistance for administrative support staff and facilities.

The Role of the Federal Judicial Center. As already noted, the district courts should submit their plans to the Federal Judicial Center, which shall compile them and then report back to Congress within eighteen months after legislation authorizing procedural reform is enacted. Specifically, this report should indicate how many districts have implemented their plans during the first year and what those plans contain.

Congress should make available appropriate funds to the center to enable it to assist the judicial councils in each circuit to develop the model plans and to study on a continuing basis the effects of the various procedural reforms adopted by the federal district courts. The judicial center could use findings from these studies to develop new procedural suggestions from time to time. To allow it to carry out this mission, the center should be authorized to ask for and receive data from the district courts.

Congress should also provide funding for either the Federal Judicial Center or the Administrative Office of the U. S. Courts to produce a *Manual for Litigation.* Among other things, this manual would provide commentary on the plans themselves, explain the rationale behind various decisions underlying the plans, and discuss how the plans might be carried out as total, integrated packages.

The suggested manual would build upon the success of the *Manual for Multidistrict Litigation* and its successor, the *Manual for Complex Litigation* (Second Edition). The idea behind the original manual was, of course, the belief that complex cases require active judicial management and that a manual could set forth the basic management tools as well as provide commentary on what experience had taught about the effective use of those tools. The *Manual for Complex Litigation* has indeed become a valuable repository of learning.

Litigation not currently covered by the existing manual can benefit from an analogous repository of experience and recommendations. Courts are experimenting energetically with various management tools, together and in combination. Wisdom gained from those experiments should be shared in some systematic way. A *Manual for Litigation* would perform that function.

PROCEDURAL RECOMMENDATION 2 : *Include in each district court's plan a system of case tracking or differentiated case management.*

The task force believes that the time has come for all federal district courts to channel cases according to their particular needs and characteristics. Many state and local courts already do this. Accordingly, we recommend that each district court's plan provide for a system of case tracking or, as some have termed it, differentiated case management, whereby cases of different degrees of complexity are placed on different time tracks for discovery and trial.

Case tracking can alleviate the problems that arise when a single set of rules is applied indiscriminately to all lawsuits—when "Cadillac-style procedures" are used to process "bicycle-size lawsuits" (Rosenberg, 1984, p. 247). For many cases the large-scale discovery methods available under the rules are simply unnecessary. Case tracking can give simple cases the quick scheduling they deserve, while reserving more time for complex cases.

The Harris survey results reported earlier show overwhelming support for case tracking: 90 percent of plaintiffs' and defendants' attorneys, 89 percent of public interest litigators, 87 percent of corporate counsel, and 78 percent of federal judges support it (Louis Harris and Associates, 1989, pp. 52, 57).

While the details of the case-tracking system (that is, the number of tracks) will likely vary from district to district, each tracking system must implement two interrelated procedures: establishing early, firm trial dates, and imposing time limits on the discovery process, directed toward completion of discovery, with related limits on the resolution of motions (Procedural Recommendations 3 and 6 below). The reason for this linkage is clear: the early completion of discovery can be counterproductive if the trial is then long delayed. The task force expects that districts would nevertheless develop different approaches suitable to their case mix; for example, different numbers of tracks and different time limits.

The New Jersey System. The state of New Jersey has experimented with a three-tiered case-tracking system that can help serve as a model for federal district court reform:

Track One is for "simple" or "expedited" cases—cases that require little or no judicial intervention prior to trial and that can be resolved in fairness to all parties within a relatively short time.

Track Two is for "complex" cases—cases that need early and intense judicial involvement.

Track Three is for "standard" cases—cases that do not fall into the other two categories.

Expanding Case Intake Information. To promote case tracking, a plan could require plaintiffs' attorneys to identify at the time the complaint is filed the track to which they believe their case should be assigned. This identification could be done through an expanded civil cover sheet, which the clerk of the court would use in making the initial assignment. If counsel for the defendant believed a different track applied, counsel could have the opportunity to so indicate within a short period. Disputes over the track assignment could and should be resolved at the initial scheduling conference (discussed in Procedural Recommendation 7). Case tracking would probably work best where courts named a "track coordinator" within the clerk's office to place cases on their respective tracks.

The Importance of Time Limits. Case tracking requires that time limits apply to each track. Judges would apply these deadlines in the "typical" case falling within each track to various stages of the litigation: for the completion of discovery, for dispositive and other key motions (motions to dismiss and for summary judgment, in particular), and for trial. Each district, through consultation between the court and the bar, can develop the standards that best suit its caseload and docket demands.

The task force believes that time limits can go a long way toward improving overall case management by attorneys and judges, reducing discovery abuse and lowering litigation transactions costs. As two legal experts have stated:

> Standards development forces judges, administrators, lawyers and others to examine what they believe is an appropriate time from filing to disposition, how rapidly most lawyers are able to prepare for trial, and how soon a court should provide a trial. While it is never possible to wholly divorce such discussions from the current pace of litigation in the jurisdiction, the sincere deliberations of concerned professionals in the system will result in goals that reflect what speedy and just disposition should mean in that jurisdiction. It is precisely this consultation that has the greatest likelihood of changing the expectations of the "local legal culture" (Solomon and Somerlot, 1987, p. 17).

A recent study by the National Center for State Courts reached a similar conclusion, finding that while time standards are

> not a panacea, . . . they can be an important part of a comprehensive program to reduce or prevent delays. First, they express an important concept: that timely disposition of the courts' business is a responsibility of the judiciary. Second, they provide goals for the court and the participants in the litigation process to seek to achieve, both in managing their total caseloads and in handling their individual cases. Third, they can lead directly to the development of systems

for monitoring caseload status and the progress of individual cases, as participants in the process seek to manage their dockets more effectively in order to achieve their goals (Mahoney, 1988, p. 63).

The General Accounting Office has confirmed these findings (U.S. GAO, 1981). After reviewing 782 files on cases that took a year or more to terminate in nine federal district courts, the GAO found the establishment and enforcement of time standards for different stages of the cases to be the critical factor in effective case management. These findings led the GAO to recommend that the Federal Rules of Civil Procedure be amended to include maximum time limits (with waivers in exceptional cases) for the various steps in the civil process.

Our recommendation is in the same spirit but is more flexible. Rather than suggesting a uniform set of time standards for all cases and for all districts, we believe each district can best set its own guidelines for time standards for the tracks it identifies. Individual judges should then apply those guideline time frames to individual cases, allowing variations only in exceptional circumstances.

PROCEDURAL RECOMMENDATION 3 : *Require in each district's tracking system the setting of early, firm trial dates at the outset of all noncomplex cases.*

The task force believes that except for cases categorized as "complex," trial dates should be set at the outset of the litigation at a mandatory scheduling conference, which should be held, in all but the simplest of cases, within at most 45 days following the first responsive pleading to the complaint (see also Procedural Recommendation 7). For "complex" cases, whose length and intricacy can often frustrate attempts to set trial schedules too far in advance, we recommend that a discovery cutoff date be fixed at the mandatory initial conference. Thereafter, within some period (say 120 days) before the discovery cutoff, the trial judge could be required to set dates for resolution of dispositive motions and trial.

Each district should consider whether trial dates should be set by day, week, or month. That decision may depend on whether the case is a jury or nonjury matter. For example, it may be that jury trials are better set by the month, while nonjury trials are better set for a date certain.

Some courts already set early and firm trial dates. Indeed, subsection (b) of Rule 16, as amended in 1983, authorizes the practice. The task force has concluded, however, that a *systemwide* requirement must be implemented. As Wayne Brazil, a leading procedural expert, has written, "fixing early and firm dates for the completion of trial preparation and for the trial itself is probably the single most effective device thus far developed for encouraging prompt and well-focused case development" (Brazil, 1981, p. 917). Professor E. Donald Elliott suggests why:

> Perhaps the most important single element of effective managerial judging is to set a firm trial date. Limiting the amount of time before trial establishes a "zero sum game," in which part of the cost of working on one issue is the opportunity cost of not being able to work on other issues within the limited time available before trial. This creates incentives for attorneys to establish priorities and "narrow the areas of inquiry and advocacy to those they believe are truly relevant and material" and to "reduce the amount of resources invested in litigation" (Elliott, 1986, pp. 313–14; citations omitted).

A 1986 American Bar Association publication also sets forth several reasons "why judges, lawyers and academics all agree" on the importance of setting firm trial dates. Such a procedure:

—dramatically increases settlement probabilities;

—eliminates duplicative preparation of witnesses when trials are rescheduled;

—is cost-effective for the trial attorney because it allows efficient and predictable scheduling of the only commodity the attorney has to sell, time; and

—requires more serious planning by the court.

The statements of these commentators are borne out in the Harris survey, which found strong support among all respondent groups for "scheduling early and firm trial dates": 79 percent of the plaintiffs' litigators, 76 percent of defendants' and public interest litigators, 85 percent of the corporate counsel, and 89 percent of the federal judges agreed with this view (Louis Harris and Associates, 1989, p. 55).

PROCEDURAL RECOMMENDATION 4 : *Set time guidelines for the completion of discovery in each district's tracking system.*

The task force recommends that each track within the district's system should provide time guidelines not only for trials but also for the completion of discovery. Using the example of the three-track system noted previously, the "expedited" track might have a discovery guideline of 50–100 days, the "standard" track a guideline of 100–200 days for the completion of discovery, and the "complex" track a discovery guideline of six to eighteen months.

The task force nevertheless recognizes that in complex cases, it may not be practicable to set a discovery time limit during the initial phase of the litigation because it may not be possible to foresee accurately when the parties ought to complete discovery. In such cases the court should establish clear intermediate targets at the outset of the litigation and should plan on identifying a fixed, final discovery cutoff date at some later point.

Many efforts have been made in the past to amend the rules to address discovery abuse. In 1980, for example, a new paragraph (f) was added to Rule 26 to put into place a two-pronged mechanism for holding discovery conferences. As a complement to that change, a new paragraph (g) was added to Rule 37 to authorize the court to award to parties who attempt to frame a discovery plan the expenses incurred in that attempt if any party or his attorney fails to participate in good faith and thereby causes additional expense. In 1983 a new paragraph was added to Rule 26(b)(1) to provide for limits on the "frequency or extent or use of the discovery methods" under certain circumstances. In addition, substantial changes were made to Rule 16 to expand the use of the scheduling conference.

Unfortunately, these well-intentioned amendments have not adequately regulated the discovery process. The task force believes that presumptive time limits for the completion of discovery— implemented as part of an overall case management system—can provide needed controls to a discovery process that is out of control. Such limits can encourage litigants and their lawyers to narrow their areas of inquiry to those they truly believe are relevant and material; to better establish discovery priorities and thus to do the most important work first; and to devote more attention to weighing the value of uncovering every single item of "relevant" material against the value of resolving the dispute fairly, quickly, and inexpensively. At the same time, time limits can give judges ammunition to discipline parties that "hide the ball" in discovery and thus force opposing counsel to seek the volumes of irrelevant material, about which many parties now complain.

Staged Discovery. Courts can accelerate the disposition of cases by "staging" discovery, which can take a variety of forms. One approach, pioneered by Judge Robert F. Peckham, limits the parties in the first stage to developing information needed for a realistic assessment of the case, perhaps by inspecting a few documents and taking a few depositions. If the case does not end, a second, more detailed stage would begin. As Judge Peckham, chief judge for the Northern District of California, explains:

> The telescoping of the discovery process will not interfere with the parties' ability to obtain full discovery if needed for trial preparation on every cause of action pleaded; it will, however, streamline costs and minimize delay by initially providing the parties only that information needed to evaluate intelligently the strengths and weaknesses of their cases. The goal of two-tiered discovery is to decrease the exorbitant costs associated with full-blown discovery by disposing of cases before reaching the second stage of discovery (Peckham, 1985, p. 269).

The Southern District of New York has used another form of staged discovery relating specifically to its interrogatory practice. Under this procedure, the parties initially are limited to issuing "identification" interrogatories—requesting the names of individuals with knowledge of the subject matter of the action, information relating to the computation of damages, and information regarding the location, custodian, and description of relevant documents. Thereafter, additional interrogatories are permitted only by leave of court. The task force believes that in determining whether to adopt such a two-stage interrogatory procedure, courts should consider both the efficiency gained from such a procedure and the equities in scaling back the availability of interrogatories, which are the least expensive discovery device available to individual plaintiffs.

Staged Disposition of Issues. The staged disposition of issues by judicial rulings can also be productive. Narrowing the contested legal or factual issues at a rapid pace can pave the way for more expeditious discovery and even settlement. Thus, courts should be encouraged, where appropriate, to manage discovery and decide motions with a view toward early resolution of key issues—for example, disputes over the length and applicability of a relevant statute of limitation, issues of contract interpretation, and so on. Often a dispute can be resolved quickly and inexpensively once a core issue is decided. Courts might also be encouraged, where appropriate, to bifurcate issues for trial, asking the jury to decide liability before damage issues, or vice versa, in torts cases, for example.

PROCEDURAL RECOMMENDATION 5 : *Permit in each district's plan only narrowly drawn "good cause" exceptions for delaying trials and discovery deadlines.*

The objectives of setting early, firm trial dates can be easily defeated if attorneys are freely permitted to obtain continuances. Thus the task force recommends that each plan include a stringent "good cause" justification for delaying trials and discovery dead lines. Importantly, each district should adopt a firm and consistent policy for minimizing continuances.

One possible model for such a policy is set forth in Section 2.55 of the American Bar Association's Standards Relating to Court Delay Reduction (1984), which provides:

Requests for continuances and extensions, and their disposition, should be recorded in the file of the case. Where continuances and extensions are requested with excessive frequency or on insubstantial grounds, the court should adopt one or a combination of the following procedures:

(1) Cross-referencing all requests for continuances and extensions by the name of the lawyer requesting them.

(2) Requiring that requests for continuances and stipulations for extensions be endorsed in writing by the litigants as well as the lawyer.

(3) Summoning lawyers who persistently request continuances and extensions to warn them of the possibility of sanctions and to encourage them to make necessary adjustment in management of their practice. Where such measures fail, restrictions may properly be imposed on the number of cases in which the lawyer may participate at any one time.

PROCEDURAL RECOMMENDATION 6 : *Include procedures for resolving motions necessary to meet the trial dates and the discovery deadlines in each district's plan.*

The task force believes that a major cause of delay is the failure by judges to decide on a timely basis fully briefed motions, whether they relate to simple discovery matters or involve requests for summary judgment. In many cases, motions that would streamline the litigation are filed early on. These motions are fully briefed and then remain undecided for an inordinate amount of time. While the parties wait for the decision, they are forced to conduct discovery on the claims or defenses that are the subject of the motion, only to find once a decision is finally rendered that the discovery was unnecessary. The result: needless and often substantial costs are incurred.

To alleviate this situation, the task force recommends that standard periods be developed and implemented for the disposition of motions. These periods would be designed to allow the parties to meet the trial dates and discovery deadlines.

The task force also recommends that each plan include a method for redressing the court's failure to decide pending motions. For example, a procedure might be developed whereby judges are obliged to report to counsel at a status conference, or otherwise, concerning such delays. We also believe that each district planning group should consider mechanisms by which the chief judge can better monitor the periods within which motions are decided.

PROCEDURAL RECOMMENDATION 7 : *Provide in each district court's plan for neutral evaluation procedures and mandatory scheduling or case management conferences at the outset of all but the simplest of cases.*

Much unnecessary cost and delay can be avoided at the outset of many cases through sensible case management evaluation and scheduling techniques. We have two specific recommendations in this area to offer.

Neutral Evaluation and Alternative Dispute Resolution. First, we suggest that each district court's plan require parties at the outset of all but the simplest and most routine cases to attend a conference with a neutral court representative to assess the suitability and desirability of alternative dispute resolution (ADR) procedures.[3] This would expand the procedures now being used in the Northern District of California, where volunteer attorneys meet with parties at an early stage to shape the issues and the discovery process.

Interest in a variety of ADR techniques has accelerated in recent years and covers a wide range of procedural devices: arbitration, mediation, and nonbinding summary trials in which the attorneys present brief summaries of their cases to juries without live testimony. Although much research remains to be done about the effectiveness of these techniques and about the circumstances to which specific ADR procedures best apply, there is some anecdotal evidence that ADR can help resolve disputes more quickly and at less cost than traditional litigation. Accordingly, we believe that the cost savings from early neutral evaluation outweigh any small additional costs of the procedure at the "front end" of litigations.

Nevertheless, because the evidence on ADR is far from definitive and because the optimal choice of specific ADR techniques varies from case to case, it would be a mistake to freeze into the procedural rules one or more particular techniques. Thus districts should experiment with ADR procedures through the neutral evaluation mechanism. In effect, we suggest that the district plans formalize the "multidoor courthouse" concept that has been imple-

3. Possible exceptions might involve various classes of administrative disputes that contribute significantly to crowded dockets in certain federal courts; for example, cases involving social security and disability claims, veterans' claims, and student loan defaults.

mented in certain federal districts and state courts. Congress should make funds available to districts to experiment with different ADR mechanisms, with a body designated to administer the funding program. As part of its ongoing assessment, the Federal Judicial Center should, in consultation with the districts, evaluate the results of these experiments and, where appropriate, suggest their regular use among all districts.

Scheduling Conferences. Once it is clear after the neutral evaluation process that a case will not be resolved through ADR, it is essential that the courts intervene at the earliest possible stage to structure the litigation with a view toward minimizing costs and delays. We believe the best mechanism for accomplishing this objective is to require each district court's plan to provide for a *mandatory* scheduling conference—presided over by judges and not magistrates—at the outset of all but the simplest and most routine of cases (the same categories of cases exempted from the neutral evaluation process would be exempted from the conference requirement). As Judge Peckham has observed, a "fairly prompt status conference prods lawyers to prepare themselves and sets the tenor of the entire litigation, by making it clear at the outset that the judge will take an active interest in the management of his cases" (Peckham, 1981, p. 785). In less complex cases, this conference could be done by telephone or as a "paper conference."

Courts should use the initial conference to set firm trial dates (except in those "complex" cases where setting a trial date would not be feasible); schedules for discovery (staged where appropriate); discovery cutoff dates within the guidelines for the particular tracks to which cases have been assigned; dates for resolving substantive and discovery motions; and dates for resolving any disputes as to the tracking category to which cases should be assigned. The initial conference can allow these schedules to be set because it educates the judge at the inception of the litigation about the nature and magnitude of the dispute.

Concerns about Judicial Management. The task force recognizes that there have been criticisms of the kind of active judicial case management or, as some have put it, "managerial judging," advocated here (Resnik, 1982). While recognizing that such critiques raise valid concerns, we conclude that judicial case management can be pursued without sacrificing the fundamental due process objectives that we all share. We concur in the compelling conclusion of Judge Alvin B. Rubin, who has written:

> The judicial role is not a passive one. A purely adversarial system, uncontrolled by the judiciary, is not an automatic guarantee that justice will be done. It is impossible to consider seriously the vital elements of a fair trial without considering that it is the duty of the judge, and the judge alone, as the sole representative of the public interest, to step in at any stage of the litigation where . . . intervention is necessary in the interest of justice. Judge Learned Hand wrote, "a judge is more than a moderator; he is charged to see that the law is properly administered, and it is a duty which he cannot discharge by remaining inert" (Rubin, 1978, p. 136).

The task force believes that its recommendations for increased judicial case management articulate an approach to the twin problems of cost and delay that maintains the essential requirements of due process. It is also noteworthy that the substantial majority of those who participate in the civil justice system, evidenced by the responses to the Harris survey (pp. 50, 54–55), overwhelmingly support active judicial management. More than eight out of ten members of the litigating bar and judges surveyed said that they favor "the concept of increasing the role of federal judges as active case managers." Roughly nine out of ten respondents specifically expressed support for "*requiring* early discovery conferences soon after the case is filed" and for "more active use of pretrial and status conferences to monitor and limit discovery."

PROCEDURAL RECOMMENDATION 8 : *Require in each district's plan that authorized representatives of the parties with decisionmaking authority be present or available by telephone during any settlement conference.*

Based on its collective litigation experience, the task force believes that cases are more likely to be settled when the clients themselves are present, in person or by telephone, during any court-sponsored settlement conference. The presence of the client makes it impossible for the attorneys to delay settlement discussions, often for weeks or months, with the time-honored excuse, "Let me get back to you after I've discussed this with my client."

In fact, Rule 16(a)(5) currently authorizes district courts to conduct a conference with the "attorneys for the parties and any unrepresented parties" for the purpose of "facilitating the settlement of the case." There is some dispute, however, over the powers district courts should have to order clients to be present at a settlement conference.

The most expansive view was recently taken in *G. Heilman Brewing Co.* v. *Joseph Oat Corp.*, 871 F. 2d 648 (1989), where a majority of the U.S. Court of Appeals for the Seventh Circuit affirmed a district court ruling assessing a sanction of costs and fees on a party who violated the court's pretrial conference order by failing to send a corporate representative with authority to settle. The majority relied on the "inherent authority" of the district court to manage its docket, acknowledging that while the district court could not compel settlement, it could compel the parties to *discuss* settlement in a neutral forum.

The dissent in *Heilman* objected to the requirement that client representatives be *physically present* at the settlement conference, arguing that litigants do not have a duty to settle their cases in "good faith." The dissent pointed to inherent difficulties in some cases in identifying the person(s) "with authority to settle."

The task force recognizes that there are practical difficulties in identifying such persons, particularly in mass tort cases (in which one attorney often represents many clients), in commercial cases in which the board of directors has the necessary decisionmaking authority, or in cases in which the client is the federal government. Nevertheless, even in these cases, *some* person or body ultimately has decisionmaking authority. Recognizing that it may be impractical and burdensome in every case to require that person or body to be physically present at a settlement conference, we recommend instead that each district plan require "authorized representatives of the parties, including counsel, with decisionmaking authority" to be present or available by telephone during any settlement conference. Congress would also be advised to consider whether statutory authorization for this practice is necessary.

PROCEDURAL RECOMMENDATION 9 : *Shorten current service provisions from 120 to 60 days.*

The task force believes that the current provision in the rules that allows 120 days for the service of process is unnecessarily long and recommends that it be shortened to 60 days. This change would accelerate the scheduling of the initial alternative dispute resolution and mandatory status conferences (see Procedural Recommendation 7).

PROCEDURAL RECOMMENDATION 10 : *Provide in each district's plan for the regular publication of pending undecided motions and caseload progress.*

To increase the likelihood that the time periods for the disposition of motions (see Procedural Recommendation 6) are followed, the task force believes that mechanisms must be developed to enhance judicial accountability. Accordingly, we recommend that the Administrative Office of the U.S. Courts be directed to computerize, in each district, the court's docket so that quarterly reports can be made to the public of at least all pending submitted motions before each judge that are unresolved for more than 30, 60, and 90 days, and all succeeding 30-day increments. In addition, courts should report data for each judge indicating the aging of his or her caseload in each of the tracking categories developed by the district. To facilitate this reporting, the Administrative Office should standardize court procedures for categorizing or characterizing judicial actions; for example, defining what is a "dismissal" and how long a case has been "pending." We believe that substantially expanding the availability of public information about caseloads by judge will encourage judges with significant backlogs in undecided motions and cases to resolve those matters and to move their cases along more quickly.

PROCEDURAL RECOMMENDATION 11 : *Ensure in each district's plan that magistrates do not perform tasks best performed by the judiciary.*

Magistrates can and do fulfill a valuable function in alleviating judges' work loads by performing many critical nonjudicial tasks, especially for routine litigation. At the same time, however, the task force believes that a number of federal district courts are relying too heavily on magistrates in civil cases to conduct certain tasks that are properly reserved to judges. It may be tempting to justify such a trend on the ground that judges in some courts are simply too overburdened with their heavy caseloads to manage their cases with the degree of attention and care they would like. But such a justification fails.

For one thing, the notion that by assuming core judicial functions magistrates can economize on judicial resources is fundamentally flawed. Decisions by magistrates on matters of importance—for example, summary judgment motions—are often appealed to the supervising judge, requiring the parties to brief and argue the same questions twice. In addition, active judicial management of cases can prevent lengthy disputes between counsel for the parties before magistrates over minor procedural issues.

Accordingly, the task force believes that each district's plan should ensure that magistrates are not performing functions that are better left to judges. In addition, district judges utilizing magistrates should be required to monitor the number of matters pending before each magistrate and how long each matter has been pending.

PROCEDURAL RECOMMENDATION 12 : *Include mechanisms for reducing backlogs in the plans of district courts with significant backlogs.*

One potential stumbling block to the development of the plans is that some districts may have serious case backlog problems. Such districts will have to develop a transition program to address these backlogs. At a minimum, such a program must include an assessment of the current backlog problem; an analysis of current judicial productivity; possible revision of current local rules to address the backlog; and a schedule for terminating the transition program, with interim goals leading to the full implementation of the district's Civil Justice Reform Plan.

Districts could address their backlogs by convening status conferences on all cases of a certain age (two years) and then imposing discovery cutoff and trial dates. In addition, courts with backlogs should experiment with "settlement weeks," such as those tried in the Superior Court for the District of Columbia.

RECOMMENDATIONS
FOR EXPANDING
JUDICIAL RESOURCES

No package of procedural reform proposals can produce meaning-ful change without the active participation of a modern, well-supported, and well-trained judiciary. Although the United States can be proud of the generally high quality of its judges, the support we give our judiciary leaves much to be desired.

Specifically, given the importance and magnitude of their re-sponsibilities, our judges are underpaid and the administrative support they receive is far from sufficient. In addition, computer facilities in many courts lag far behind the equipment and person-nel available to the private bar. No case-tracking system can work efficiently unless the computer facilities and data base systems are in place to track the progress of all the cases in each district.

The task force believes that with a relatively modest amount of additional funds—several hundred million dollars, at most—the federal judicial system can be readied for the twenty-first century, both in terms of administrative support and salary levels for the judges who are the centerpieces of our judicial system.

JUDICIAL RESOURCE RECOMMENDATION 1 : *Expand adminis-trative support.*

Each district court has different resource needs, whether simply to keep pace with current litigation or to make the improvements in the civil justice system that we believe are desirable and neces-sary. Accordingly, we propose that at the time each district submits its plan to the Federal Judicial Center it also submit to Congress a report indicating by how much the plan seeks to reduce cost and delay and what additional resources—including administrative staff, computer facilities, and software support—are required to achieve the announced objectives. This process should educate

Congress, the executive branch, and the public in general about the relatively modest additional resource requirements for making the substantial improvements in the civil justice system that we believe can be made.

We further recommend that Congress make available some funds for additional staff and computer support at the same time that it requests the district courts to develop their plans. These funds should be directed only to those districts that develop and implement the plans.

JUDICIAL RESOURCE RECOMMENDATION 2 : *Expand judicial case management training programs.*

The proposed case-tracking system and related recommendations designed to improve judicial case management require judges themselves to be effective case managers. Given the wide variety of professional backgrounds and experiences of federal district court judges, many judges may find it useful to become familiar with the case management techniques being used throughout the country. In particular, there are many judges now on the bench who have experimented successfully with various procedural approaches. In addition, there are law professors and other independent experts on judicial management who have examined which of the many techniques now in use are likely to be most effective in resolving disputes quickly and fairly. The accumulated learning on this subject needs to be better transmitted throughout the federal judiciary. Moreover, with the development and implementation of the plans recommended in this report, now information   descriptive and statistical—will be generated.

Accordingly, the task force recommends that current judicial training programs be expanded to include a new curriculum and emphasis on efficient case management and that funding be made available to make this possible.

JUDICIAL RESOURCE RECOMMENDATION 3 : *Fill judicial vacancies and review the need for additional judges.*

It is likely that many, if not most, districts with substantial case backlogs will request additional judges as a principal means of cutting delay. The task force believes that some pressure for more judges can be relieved through procedural reform, as already discussed. Nevertheless, we also believe that more judges in certain districts might be required if the backlog problem is to be adequately addressed. Moreover, various districts have been waiting for additional federal judges, who have yet to be nominated by the Department of Justice. The task force urges the administration to fill these vacancies expeditiously.

JUDICIAL RESOURCE RECOMMENDATION 4 : *Increase judicial salaries.*

The foregoing recommendations make clear that costs and delay in the federal courts can be reduced only through the active involvement of the federal judiciary. In many cases, judges may have to work even harder than they do now, when as a group they are already burdened by heavy caseloads.

Clearly, it is only fair, and indeed long overdue, that the salaries of federal judges be significantly increased. The task force recognizes this is a highly emotional issue, as the public outcry over the proposed congressional and federal employee pay increase in early 1989 attests. But the issue must be addressed, and soon. While lifetime judgeships carry prestige and security, it is short-sighted of society to expect that America's best attorneys will continue to be attracted to the judiciary when, as practicing lawyers, they can earn substantially greater sums. Adjusted for inflation, federal judicial salaries have fallen 30 percent during the past twenty years (Hedges, 1989). As a result, judicial salaries have badly lagged behind those for practicing attorneys. Indeed, graduating law students can now earn in law firms in New York City *in their first year* as much as a federal judge. Elsewhere around the country, it takes only several years out of law school for attorneys to do the same.

Inadequate judicial salaries have already led some federal district judges to return to the private sector. Members of the task force know of highly qualified lawyers who have turned down potential appointments because of the salary. If this trend continues, the nation faces a real threat that many of its best federal judges will leave the bench for private practice, and many more highly qualified potential judges will be discouraged from taking on judicial responsibilities.

This possibility must not be allowed to occur. The task force recommends that Congress move quickly to provide substantial pay increases to federal judges.

RECOMMENDATIONS FOR CLIENTS AND THEIR ATTORNEYS

Although the civil justice system must be structured to provide incentives for the participants to resolve their disputes quickly and inexpensively, clients and their attorneys must also respond to those incentives. We do not pretend to have all the answers about how these responses are best made. But we agree that several steps are appropriate.

RECOMMENDATIONS FOR THE BAR

The task force's procedural recommendations focus to a large degree on steps that courts and judges should take to reduce litigation costs and delays. But still more will be needed to make significant improvements in our civil justice system. The nation needs—and must get—a substantial commitment from the bar to address this challenge as well.

The legal profession has changed dramatically during the last decade or more: law has evolved from a profession to a business, one that is increasingly dominated by escalating attorney salaries, heavier demands for billable hours, and diminished loyalty among firm partners. Sol Linowitz has aptly described this state of affairs:

> Over the years . . . something seriously disturbing has been happening to the legal profession. We have become a business—dominated by "bottom line" perspectives. In too many of our law firms, the computer has become the Managing Partner as we are ruled by hourly rates, time sheets and electronic devices. We have seen an increase in technological expertise with a corresponding diminution of the human side of law practice (Linowitz, 1988).

Chief Justice Rehnquist has echoed this theme:

> The practice of law in the United States has evolved from a profession to a business, with all that those terms connote: emphasis on making money, increased competition for clients, increased mobility of lawyers (Rehnquist, 1988).

This change in the structure of the profession—especially the emphasis on higher billable hours—has noticeably affected the conduct of litigation, most specifically in the area of discovery. For example, in the Harris survey, strong majorities of each respondent group identified "lawyers and litigants who use discovery as an adversarial tool or tactic to raise the stakes for their opponents" as a major cause of litigation costs and delays: 64 percent of defense litigators, 71 percent of public interest litigators, 77 percent of corporate counsel, and 71 percent of federal trial judges shared this view. In addition, 40 percent of the defense litigators and 46 percent of their counterparts from the plaintiffs' bar indicated that "lawyers who use discovery and motion practice simply to drive up the bill" were a major cause of costs and delays. Finally, 38 percent of the defense litigators and 44 percent of the plaintiffs' litigators indicated that "counsel who keep cases alive as long as possible to maximize billings" were another major cause of costs and delays (Louis Harris and Associates, 1989, p. 25).

In short, there is a consensus that some litigation costs are not demanded by the merits of the case, but rather are incurred as a direct outgrowth of the incentives that have been built into the private legal industry itself. The task force believes that the time has come for the profession to examine the impact of costs on the delivery of legal services and the critical question whether increasing costs have impeded access to the courts.

More important, the profession must devote more resources to lowering the costs of litigation, in money and in time. The fact that our group, consisting of a broad range of participants in the legal system with widely different views on matters of substantive law, was able to agree upon some basic cost-reducing measures demonstrates that change is possible. The organized bar ought to encourage more of these kinds of interchanges throughout the country.

Our recommendation that planning groups be formed in each federal district to develop expense and time reduction plans, if followed, would stimulate such meetings.

Fortunately, some efforts are already under way. The task force identified a number of positive steps that many attorneys and their firms have already taken. Many firms, for example, are giving clients litigation budgets and strategic plans at the outset of their cases so that they can anticipate the ultimate cost. Firms also underwrite, through the National Institute of Trial Advocacy programs, the training of attorneys to help them select winning from losing cases and to avoid unnecessary discovery.

RECOMMENDATIONS FOR CLIENTS

The group focused almost entirely on what large corporate clients could do to reduce transaction costs. Two broad approaches are being tried: bringing more litigation "in-house" and exercising greater supervision over outside counsel (see Banks, 1983).

While the data are sparse, hiring in-house counsel to conduct routine, and often highly repetitive, litigation appears to reduce costs. As a recent article in the *American Bar Association Journal* points out:

> In-house lawyers have no incentive to bill unnecessary hours, do not need to be educated about the corporation's business, know how to locate witnesses and documents quickly, tend not to engage in excessive memo writing or redrafting, are not pulled off a matter for another client's crisis and, in general, do not feel obliged to create a Cadillac work product to impress a partner when a Chevrolet will do the job (Machlowitz, 1989, p. 66).

A recent survey by Arthur Young finds that major corporations are rapidly bringing their litigation in-house. In 1983 only 37 percent of those surveyed indicated that they handled at least some of their litigation internally. By 1987 that number had increased to 75 percent (Dockser, 1988).

To handle the increased volume of in-house work, corporations have been luring away prominent litigators and senior partners from private law firms. This trend should help hold down litigation costs, since corporate counsel who were previously affiliated with private law firms are in an ideal position to monitor and control the costs of outside counsel.

Of course, there are limits to cost savings from moving legal work in-house. Businesses will continue to use private law firms for nonregular and complex litigation requiring specialized expertise. In addition, outside counsel may continue to be required where the behavior of top corporate officials may be at issue.

But even where corporations must look to outside lawyers for representation, we believe that they can do a better job of supervision and cost control. Several supervisory techniques that some corporations are now using are likely to be successful:

—Increasing corporate counsel's involvement in case management by specifying guidelines for outside attorneys; developing trial books or manuals for acceptable litigation techniques and tactics; requiring the presence of corporate counsel at trial; developing computer-based case-tracking systems that allow corporations to follow day-to-day litigation actions.

—Using these computerized systems or other techniques to develop cost data on routine cases and using that data to develop litigation budgets; taking competitive bids for certain work.

—Insisting upon litigation budgets and litigation plans at the outset of a case.

—Encouraging the use of more paralegals and other nonlawyers for reading and summarizing files and documents.

—Appointing corporate record supervisors to monitor and facilitate record production.

These are only a sampling of the techniques that were raised in the group's discussions or appear in the literature. General counsel also spoke of different goals in supervision. Some saw the supervisory function as primarily review of bills and unnecessary staff (for example, the assignment of several associates to a case where one partner would do). Others believed that the key objective of supervision is to encourage early settlement. Most believed both goals are essential.

At bottom, companies should evaluate each case to determine whether it could be defended or pursued more efficiently in-house or outside. All cases, however, must be managed and not simply handed off by default to the responsible attorney. This prescription applies to all clients, whether large or small.

FURTHER AGENDA

Our efforts to identify workable professional and client initiatives to control litigation costs suggest that much additional work remains to be done. In particular:

—A study should be undertaken to determine what other innovative cost-control techniques are being undertaken by private law firms and which, if any, of these techniques have actually reduced costs. These findings should enable the national or local bar associations to promote the use of proven techniques for reducing litigation costs and delay.

—The use of private and court-annexed alternative dispute resolution mechanisms needs more thorough study, with focus on whether ADR actually helps to reduce transaction costs.

—The changing nature of the federal civil litigation docket merits further study to determine what sorts of civil litigation are increasing in frequency and burden and what efforts, if any, might be undertaken to provide alternative and less costly resolution of these disputes.

—Much better information about corporate litigation expenditures for both inside and outside counsel must be developed. A thorough study would help reveal why litigation costs are increasing and which cost-control techniques would prove most successful. It would also be desirable to determine to what extent the movement of corporate legal functions in-house has reduced costs.

—Finally, given the public import of civil litigation costs and delay, Congress should direct the Department of Justice to include civil litigation problems on the research agenda of the National Institute of Justice, which now only studies criminal justice issues. Such a step would help launch much of the statistical research work that needs to be done if policymakers, judges, and litigants are to make intelligent choices among various methods for reducing cost and delay.

As in many areas addressed by this report the dearth of adequate data is a serious problem in developing meaningful recommendations. Many members of the task force believe that private initiatives may be as successful as the legislative recommendations outlined above in achieving sigificant reductions in litigation costs and delay. However, a firm data base is necessary to make the case to the private sector that such initiatives are cost effective. We hope that in the future the organized bar and the "client community" will significantly enhance their support for further research in this area.

BIBLIOGRAPHY

References cited in the text are listed below, in alphabetical order:

Banks, Robert S., "Companies Struggle to Control Legal Costs," *Harvard Business Review*, vol. 61 (March–April 1983), pp. 168–70.

Bok, Derek, *The President's Report, 1981–82* (Harvard University, April 1983).

Brazil, Wayne D., "Improving Judicial Controls over the Pretrial Development of Civil Actions: Model Rules for Case Management and Sanctions," *American Bar Foundation Research Journal*, no. 4 (Fall 1981), pp. 875–965.

Dockser, Amy, "Companies Rein in Outside Legal Bills," *Wall Street Journal*, November 9, 1988.

Elliott, E. Donald, "Managerial Judging and the Evolution of Procedure," *University of Chicago Law Review*, vol. 53 (Spring 1986), pp. 306–36.

Erickson, William H., "The Pound Conference Recommendations: A Blueprint for the Justice System in the Twenty-First Century," 76 F.R.D. 277 (1978).

Hedges, Stephen J., "The Quiet Crisis in America's Courts," *U.S. News and World Report*, April 3, 1989, pp. 30–31.

Linowitz, Sol M., keynote address, Cornell Law School Centennial, April 15, 1988

Louis Harris and Associates, *Procedural Reform of the Civil Justice System*, study conducted for the Foundation for Change (New York, March 1989).

Machlowitz, David S., "Lawyers Move In-House," *American Bar Association Journal*, vol. 75 (May 1989), pp. 66–69.

Mahoney, Barry, and others, *Changing Times in Trial Courts* (National Center for State Courts, 1988).

Newman, Jon O., "Rethinking Fairness: Perspectives on the Litigation Process," *Yale Law Journal*, vol. 94 (June 1985), pp. 1643–59.

Peckham, Robert F., "A Judicial Response to the Cost of Litigation: Case Management, Two-Stage Discovery Planning and Alternative Dispute Resolution," *Rutgers Law Review*, vol. 37 (Winter 1985), pp. 253–77.

———, "The Federal Judge as a Case Manager: The New Role in Guiding a Case from Filing to Disposition," *California Law Review*, vol. 69 (May 1981), pp. 770–805.

Pound, Roscoe, "The Causes of Popular Dissatisfaction with the Administration of Justice," reprinted at 35 F.R.D. 273 (1964).

Powell, Lewis, dissenting statement to *Amendments to the Federal Rules of Civil Procedure*, 85 F.R.D. 521, 522–23 (1980).

Rehnquist, William H., remarks before the Australian Bar Association, Sydney, September 3, 1988.

Resnik, Judith, "Managerial Judges," *Harvard Law Review*, vol. 96 (December 1982), pp. 374–448.

Rosenberg, Maurice, "Federal Rules of Civil Procedure in Action: Assessing Their Impact," January 1989.

———, "The Federal Civil Rules after Half a Century," *Maine Law Review*, vol. 36 (Spring 1984), pp. 242–51.

Rubin, Alvin B., "The Managed Calendar: Some Pragmatic Suggestions about Achieving the Just, Speedy, and Inexpensive Determination of Civil Cases in Federal Courts," *Justice System Journal*, vol. 4 (Winter 1978), pp. 135–46.

Schwarzer, William W., "Mistakes Lawyers Make in Discovery," *Litigation*, vol. 15 (Winter 1989), pp. 31–34, 58.

Solomon, Maureen, and Douglas K. Somerlot, *Caseflow Management in the Trial Court: Now and for the Future* (Chicago, Ill.: American Bar Association, 1987).

U.S. General Accounting Office, *Better Management Can Ease Federal Civil Case Backlog*, GGD-81-2 (February 24, 1981).

Numerous other articles and books on delay and transactions costs in the civil justice system have been published through the years. Although a complete bibliography is too long to be reproduced here, selected references include:

Brazil, Wayne D., and others, "Early Neutral Evaluation: An Experimental Effort to Expedite Dispute Resolution," *Judicature*, vol. 69 (February–March 1986), pp. 279–86.

Connolly, Paul R., Edith A. Holleman, and Michael J. Kuhlman, *Judicial Controls and the Civil Litigative Process: Discovery* (Washington: Federal Judicial Center, 1978).

Dungworth, Terence, and Nicholas M. Pace, *Statistical Overview of Civil Litigation in the Federal Courts* (Santa Monica, Calif.: Rand Corp., Institute for Civil Justice, 1989).

Flegal, Frank F., and Steven M. Umin, "Curbing Discovery Abuse in Civil Litigation: We're Not There Yet," *Brigham Young University Law Review*, no. 3 (Summer 1981), pp. 597–616.

Galanter, Marc, "The Life and Times of the Big Six; or, The Federal Courts since the Good Old Days," Working Paper Series 9 (Institute for Legal Studies, Disputes Processing Research Program, University of Wisconsin–Madison Law School, August 1988).

Kastenmeier, Robert W., and Michael J. Remington, "Court Reform and Access to Justice: A Legislative Perspective," *Harvard Journal on Legislation*, vol. 16 (Spring 1979), pp. 301–42.

Lieberman, Jethro K., and James F. Henry, "Lessons from the Alternative Dispute Resolution Movement," *University of Chicago Law Review*, vol. 53 (Spring 1986), pp. 424–39.

McGovern, Francis, "Toward a Functional Approach for Managing Complex Litigation," *University of Chicago Law Review*, vol. 53 (Spring 1986), pp. 440–93.

McMillan, Richard, Jr., and David B. Siegel, "Creating a Fast-Track Alternative under the Federal Rules of Civil Procedure," *Notre Dame Law Review*, vol. 60 (Spring 1985), pp. 431–55.

Note, "Discovery Abuse under the Federal Rules: Causes and Cures," *Yale Law Journal*, vol. 92 (December 1982), pp. 352–75.

Priest, George L., "Private Litigants and the Court Congestion Problem," Revised Working Paper 79 (Civil Liability Program, Yale Law School, July 1989).

Resnik, Judith, "Failing Faith: Adjudicatory Procedure in Decline," *University of Chicago Law Review*, vol. 53 (Spring 1986), pp. 494–560.

Zeisel, Hans, Harry Kalven, Jr., and Bernard Bucholz, *Delay in the Court* (Little, Brown, 1959).

MEMBERS OF THE TASK FORCE

The following were members of the Brookings Task Force on Civil Justice Reform:

DEBRA BALLEN is Vice President for Policy Development and Research at the American Insurance Association in Washington, D.C., where she is responsible for long-range planning on a variety of issues affecting the property-casualty insurance industry.

ROBERT BANKS is Counsel to Latham & Watkins in New York. He was formerly General Counsel of the Xerox Corporation and Chairman of the Board of the American Corporate Counsel Association.

ROBERT G. BEGAM is President of Langerman, Begam, Lewis and Marks, P.A., in Phoenix, Arizona. He has served as President of the Association of Trial Lawyers of America.

GIDEON CASHMAN is a senior partner at Pryor, Cashman, Sherman & Flynn in New York.

ALFRED W. CORTESE is a partner at Kirkland & Ellis, Washington, D.C., who has litigated numerous commercial, antitrust, tort, and products liability cases in the courts and administrative agencies. He is a former Assistant Executive Director of the Federal Trade Commission and is currently a member of the Executive Committee of Lawyers for Civil Justice.

SUSAN GETZENDANNER is a partner at Skadden, Arps, Slate, Meagher & Flom in Chicago, Illinois. She was formerly a judge in the United States District Court for the Northern District of Illinois.

MARK GITENSTEIN (Reporter) is Counsel to Mayer, Brown & Platt in Washington, D.C., and Executive Director of the Foundation for Change, Washington, D.C. He was formerly Chief Counsel to the Judiciary Committee of the U.S. Senate.

BARRY GOLDSTEIN is Director of the Washington office of the NAACP Legal Defense and Educational Fund.

JAMIE GORELICK is a partner at Miller, Cassidy, Larrocca & Lewin in Washington, D.C. She is currently Secretary to the American Bar Association's Section of Litigation and was Chair of its Committee on Complex Crimes Litigation. She has also taught trial advocacy at the Harvard Law School.

MARCIA D. GREENBERGER is the Managing Attorney of the National Women's Law Center in Washington, D.C. She founded the Women's Rights Project of the Center for Law and Social Policy and has practiced law with Caplin & Drysdale in Washington.

PATRICK HEAD is the Vice President and General Counsel of the FMC Corporation. He previously held the same position for Montgomery Ward.

DEBORAH HENSLER is Director of Research at the Institute for Civil Justice, Rand Corporation, Santa Monica, California.

W. MICHAEL HOUSE is a partner at Shaw, Pittman, Potts & Trowbridge in Washington, D.C. He was formerly Administrative Assistant to Senator Howell Heflin.

SHIRLEY HUFSTEDLER is a partner at Hufstedler, Miller, Kaus & Beardsley in Los Angeles. She formerly served as U.S. Secretary of Education, a federal judge on the United States Court of Appeals for the Ninth Circuit, and a county and state court judge in California.

KENNETH KAY is a partner at Preston, Thorgrimson, Ellis & Holman, Washington, D.C., and Executive Director of the Council on Research and Technology. He was formerly a Counsel to the Judiciary Committee of the U.S. Senate and Legislative Director for Senator Max Baucus.

GENE KIMMELMAN is the Legislative Director of the Consumer Federation of America, where he directs the federation's legislative and regulatory intervention program. He was formerly a staff attorney for Congress Watch.

NORMAN KRIVOSHA is Executive Vice President–Administration and General Counsel for Ameritas Financial Services of Lincoln, Nebraska. He was formerly the Chief Justice of the Nebraska Supreme Court.

LEO LEVIN is Leon Meltzer Professor of Law Emeritus at the University of Pennsylvania Law School, specializing in civil procedure and judicial administration. He was formerly Director of the Federal Judicial Center.

CARL D. LIGGIO is the General Counsel of Ernst & Young in New York. He was formerly Chairman of the Board of the American Corporate Counsel Association.

ROBERT E. LITAN (Reporter) is a Senior Fellow and Director of the Center for Economic Progress within the Economic Studies Program at the Brookings Institution. He is also Counsel to Powell, Goldstein, Frazer & Murphy in Washington, D.C., and a Visiting Lecturer in Banking Law at the Yale Law School.

FRANK MCFADDEN is the Senior Vice President and General Counsel of Blount, Inc. He was formerly Chief Judge of the United States District Court for the District of Alabama and he is currently Chairman of the Board of the American Corporate Counsel Association.

FRANCIS MCGOVERN is a Professor of Law at the School of Public Health, University of Alabama at Birmingham. He has served as a special master in several major cases involving toxic tort allegations.

STEPHEN B. MIDDLEBROOK is the Senior Vice President and General Counsel at Aetna Life & Casualty. He served on the American Bar Association's Action Commission to Improve the Tort Liability System and was a founder of the American Corporate Counsel Association, where he now serves on the Executive Committee.

EDWARD MULLER is Vice President, General Counsel, and Chief Administrative Officer of Whittaker Corporation. He formerly practiced law with the Washington, D.C., firm of Leva, Hawes, Symington, Martin & Oppenheimer.

ROBERT M. OSGOOD is a partner in charge of litigation, antitrust, arbitration and competition law services in the London office of Sullivan & Cromwell. He was formerly Managing Partner of the firm's Litigation Group in New York.

ALAN PARKER is Deputy Executive Director of the Association of Trial Lawyers of America. He was formerly General Counsel to the House Judiciary Committee.

RICHARD PAUL is Vice President and General Counsel of Xerox Corporation. He was previously in private law practice.

JUDYTH PENDELL is an Assistant Vice President of Law and Public Affairs at Aetna Life & Casualty, where she oversees the company's civil justice reform efforts.

JOHN A. PENDERGRASS is a Senior Attorney in the Research and Policy Analysis Division of the Environmental Law Institute. He formerly taught law at the Illinois Institute of Technology, Chicago–Kent College of Law, and practiced law in the public and private sectors.

GEORGE PRIEST is the John M. Olin Professor of Law and Economics at the Yale Law School, where he teaches torts, products liability, insurance policy, and antitrust law. He also directs the Program in Civil Liability at the Yale Law School.

CHARLES B. RENFREW is a Director and Vice President–Law of the Chevron Corporation. He was formerly a United States District Judge for the Northern District of California and Deputy Attorney General of the United States.

TONY ROISMAN is Of Counsel to Cohen, Milstein & Hausfeld, Washington, D.C. He formerly served as the Director of Trial Lawyers for Public Justice and as Chief of the Hazardous Waste Section of the Land and Natural Resources Division of the U.S. Department of Justice.

JOHN F. SCHMUTZ is the Senior Vice President and General Counsel for E.I. duPont de Nemours & Company, Wilmington, Delaware.

CHRISTOPHER SCHROEDER is a Professor of Law at the Duke University Law School, where he teaches civil procedure, environmental law, and property. Previously he practiced law with McCutchen, Doyle, Brown & Emerson and Armour, Schroeder, St. John and Wilcox, specializing in civil litigation.

BILL WAGNER is a trial lawyer in Tampa, Florida, who represents claimants in personal injury and wrongful death matters. Currently he is the President of the Association of Trial Lawyers of America.

DIANE WOOD is Associate Dean and Professor of Law at the University of Chicago Law School. Formerly she practiced law with Covington & Burling in Washington, D.C.

In addition to the above members, several individuals provided valuable assistance to the task force during its deliberations. They include:

Jeffrey Connaughton, *Special Assistant, Senate Judiciary Committee*

Terrence Dungworth, *Institute for Civil Justice, Rand Corporation*

Frank Flegal, *Professor of Law, Georgetown University Law School*

Mary Kay Kane, *Professor of Law, Hastings College of Law, University of California*

Jeffrey Peck, *General Counsel, Senate Judiciary Committee*

The Honorable Robert F. Peckham, *Chief Judge, Northern District of California*

Leonard M. Ring, *Chairman of the Torts and Insurance Practice Section of the American Bar Association and former President of the Association of Trial Lawyers of America*

Maurice Rosenberg, *Professor of Law, Columbia Law School*

The Honorable Carl Rubin, *Chief Judge, Southern District of Ohio*

Thomas J. Scheuerman, *Associate General Counsel, 3M Corporation*

Molly Selvin, *Institute for Civil Justice, Rand Corporation*